Beginner P Lessons for Kids

Book with Online Video and Audio Access

By
Jay Wamsted

For Online Video & Audio Access, go to this address on the internet:
http://cvls.com/extras/kidspiano/

About the Author

Jay Wamsted teaches high school math in southwest Atlanta. He has been playing piano for over thirty years—sometimes in bands and sometimes alone. He holds a Ph.D. in education from Georgia State University and his published writing can be found both online and in various journals and magazines. In addition to teaching math, he has taught private lessons for both piano and guitar; currently he is working with his own children on these very arrangements. Several of his original piano compositions can be streamed at Amazon Play, Apple Music, Spotify, and elsewhere.

Watch & Learn Products Really Work

Over thirty years ago, Watch & Learn revolutionized instructional music courses by developing well thought out, step-by-step methods. These courses were tested for effectiveness on beginners before publication. These lessons have continued to improve and evolve into the Watch & Learn system that continues to set the standard of music instruction today. This has resulted in sales of more than three million products since 1979.

Ode to Joy
Slow

About this Course

This course was designed for elementary school-aged children (5-12 years old) with an emphasis on getting the student to play real music as quickly as possible. Our method is unique because of two basic concepts. First, we teach songs that many kids will already know. This avoids the student becoming overwhelmed by learning rhythm notation. Secondly, the notation shows fingering for each note so students don't have to memorize note names and key positions.

The course starts with simple songs using just the right hand and gradually builds up to using both hands and more complicated rhythms. It's important for the student to know that everyone learns at a different speed. Younger children may require more guidance to work through the book. It's also important for adults to remember to encourage the student and be proud of any progress that is made.

Course Material

In addition to this book, you also have access to over an hour of video instruction that covers all of the material taught in the book. This is an important tool for helping the student play in time and with proper form.

The audio tracks demonstrate each song at two different speeds. The slower speed features just the piano playing the song. The faster version includes vocals and other instruments in a performance-like setting. Go to this address on the internet to access the video and audio tracks:

http://cvls.com/extras/kidspiano/

If you ever need any assistance accessing or using these materials, please send an email to sales@cvls.com. The tracks feature piano and vocals by Jay Wamsted. The tracks were recorded by and feature guitar and bass parts by Toby Ruckert at uTOBYa Studio.

Table of Contents

Playing with Both Hands

Bonus Information

Getting Started

For Online Video & Audio Access, go to this address on the internet:
http://cvls.com/extras/kidspiano/

Sitting Position

- Sit up straight

- Let your arms hang loosely

- Try to find a bench or chair that puts your knees just below the keys

- Do not rest your elbows on your legs as you play

- Compare your hand position and posture to these photos and to the online video

Correct Hand Position
(fingers curved)

Don't Slouch

Don't rest your elbows on your legs

Hand Position

Your fingers should never be straight - but curved - like you are holding a clementine.

Correct Hand Position
(fingers curved)

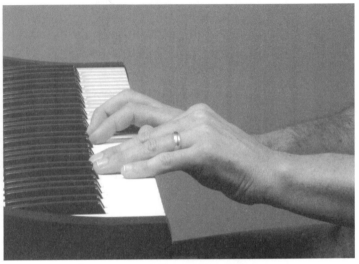

Incorrect Hand Position
(fingers straight)

Use only the tips of your fingers to strike the keys

Learning The Keys

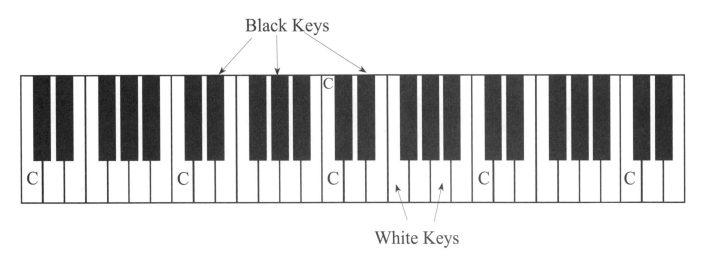

Black Keys

White Keys

Pianos have 88 keys. Electronic keyboards usually have less. You may have 76, 61 or fewer.

The keys are divided into black and white keys. For this course, we're only going to play the white keys. Our home base is called middle C. In the middle of your piano or keyboard, you'll see two black keys together. Put the thumb of your right hand on the white key that is to the left of the first black key.

Exercise 1

Find middle C and play it using your thumb. Check your note by watching the Video.

This symbol stands for middle C.

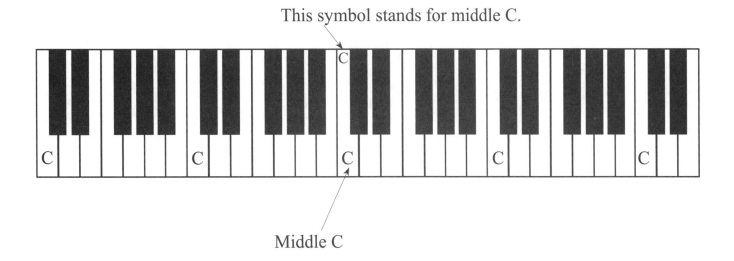

Middle C

Numbering the Fingers

We're going to give each of our right hand fingers a number name. It doesn't matter if you are right or left handed. Everyone will use their right hand to play these notes.

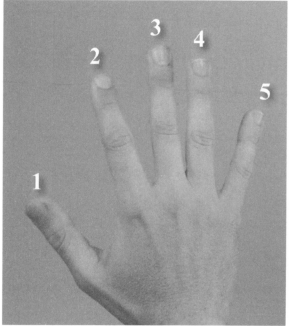

Right Hand

Exercise 2

Find middle C and then place your right thumb on it. Now play middle C and the 4 white keys to the right or up the keyboard one at a time. Use your 1st finger, 2nd finger, 3rd finger, 4th finger, and 5th finger. Play along with the video.

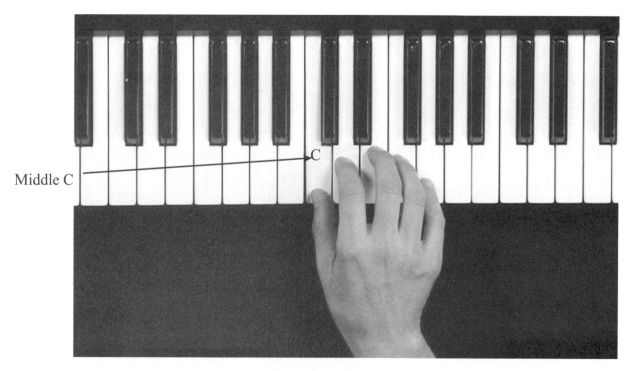

Middle C

Music Notation

Music has its own special language that tells you how to play the music. There are five lines that will have notes either on them or above or below them. We're going to add a number above each note to tell you which finger to use.

Exercise 3

Let's try playing Exercise 2 again. This time we'll look at the notation for it.

These notes also have letter names.

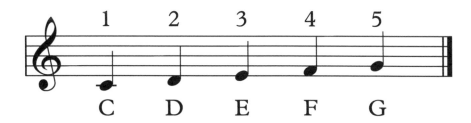

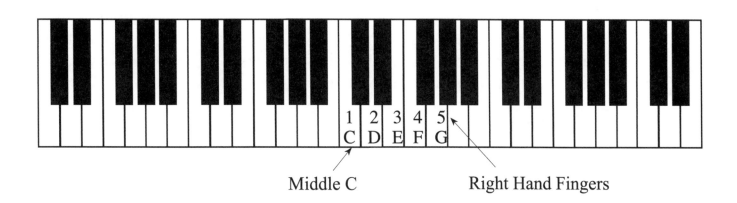

Middle C   Right Hand Fingers

As you keep playing piano, you will learn to read the note names. But for now, we'll just use the numbers.

There is a more detailed explanation of music notation starting on page 37.

Note Values

We call each set of lines a staff. We also can divide the staff into smaller sections called measures.

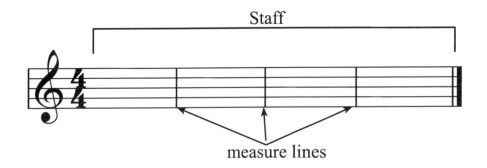

Staff

measure lines

The notation can also tell us how long to play. Think of each measure as having four beats. Count 1 2 3 4.

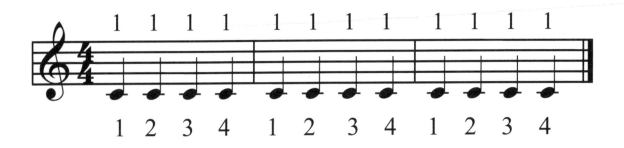

Exercise 4

Let's start by playing whole notes. Each whole note takes up a whole measure. So you'll press your thumb down for four counts

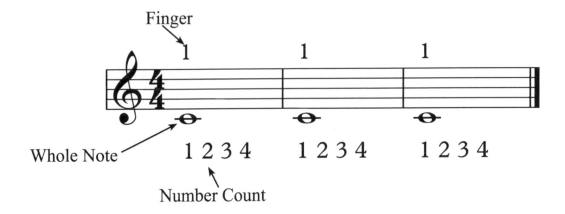

Finger

Whole Note

Number Count

6

Exercise 5

Next we'll play half notes. There are two half notes in each measure. So you'll press the key with your thumb and count "one two". Let go of the key and then press it again and count "three four".

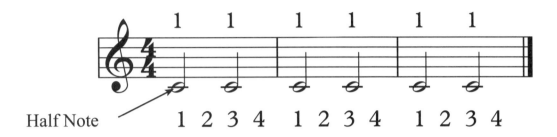

Half Note

Exercise 6

Now we'll play quarter notes. There are four quarter notes in each measure. So we'll press the key for each number we count.

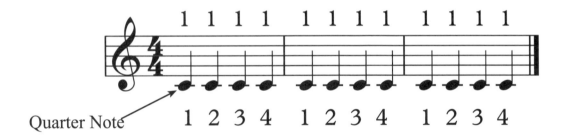

Quarter Note

Exercise 7

Play middle C, first as a whole note, then as two half notes, and finally as four quarter notes. Play along with the video.

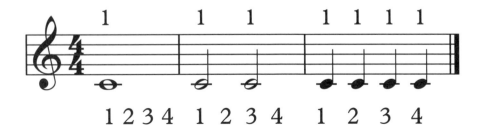

7

Practice Tips

Before we play our first song, let's talk about how to learn and practice each song.

- First, watch the video so you can see where your fingers should go and listen to the song.

- Second, practice playing the song as slowly as you need to.

- Third, try playing with the video at the slower speed.

- Once you feel comfortable, try playing along with the second or faster speed.

- If you're getting frustrated, try taking a break or practicing a different song. Learning the piano is supposed to be a fun experience.

- Don't try to practice for an hour at at time. Try practicing for ten to twenty minutes at a time once or twice a day.

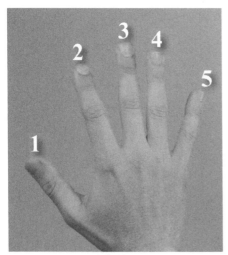

Right Hand

♩ = 1 beat

𝅗𝅥 = 2 beats

𝅝 = 4 beats

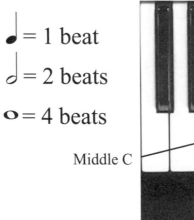

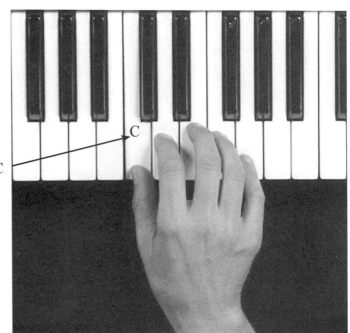

Middle C

The C Position

Place your right hand in the C Position and play along with the video. The right hand fingering is represented by the numbers. Our first song will be *Mary Had A Little Lamb*. Take it slow at first.

Mary Had A Little Lamb

Right Hand Fingering

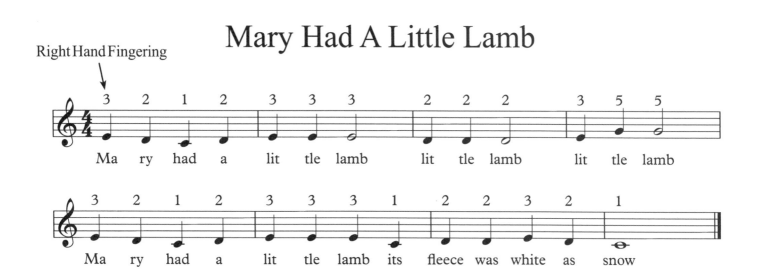

9

Most of our songs can be played in the C position we just learned. Let's try another one.

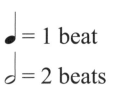

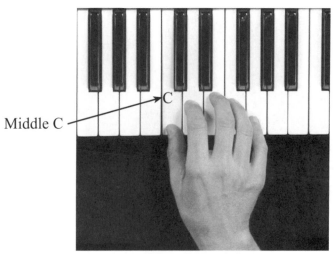

The C Position

Ode To Joy

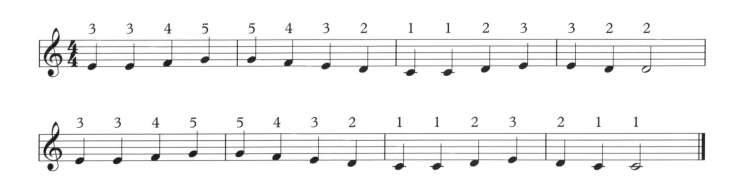

Ludwig van Beethoven

 **FUN FACT**

Beethoven was deaf when he wrote this song. Wow?

Let's do another short song. This one has 8th notes in it. They come twice as fast as quarter notes, so ♫ = ♩.

♫ = 2 half beats

♩ = 1 beat

𝅗𝅥 = 2 beats

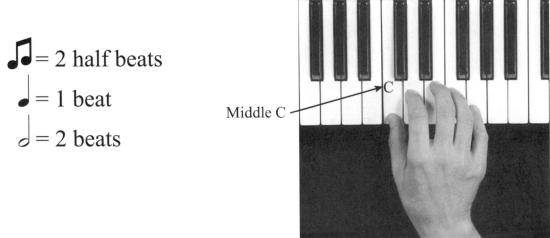

The C Position

Exercise 8

Play middle C again, first as two half notes, then as 4 quarter notes, and finally as eight eighth notes. Play along with the video.

Hot Cross Buns

Place your right hand in the C Position again to play *Hot Cross Buns*.

REMEMBER

It's ok if you make a mistake while you're playing a song. You may have to practice the song many times before your fingers remember what to do.

11

The Rest

Let's learn a longer song with two new rhythm ideas. Sometimes we want to have a beat with no music played. This symbol is a rest (𝄽). The rest means to take a break for one beat. No music! It may help to say rest aloud (1 2 3 rest).

We already know that a half note lasts 2 beats and a whole note lasts 4 beats. If we want to play 3 beats, you'll see a dotted half note (𝅗𝅥.).

Exercise 9

Let's play the dotted half note and rest in each measure and count it out.

Note - You have probably heard and sung Jingle Bells many times, but it's a little harder to play it on the piano for the first time. Try to play it slowly and then gradually speed up.

♫ = 2 half beats

♩ = 1 beat

♩ = 2 beats

♩. = 3 beats

𝅝 = 4 beats

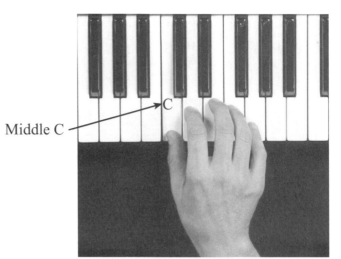

The C Position

Middle C → C

Jingle Bells

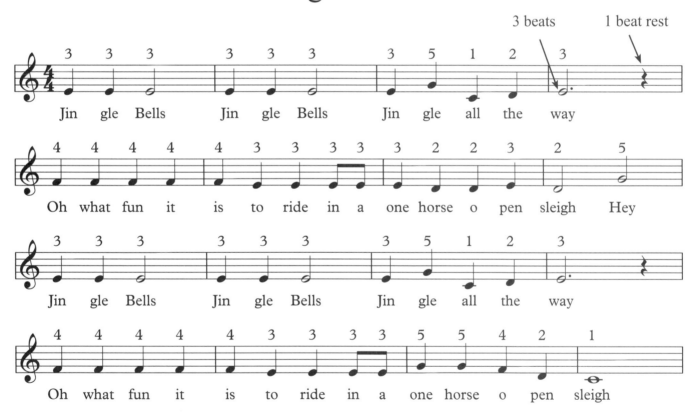

3 beats   1 beat rest

| 3 | 3 | 3 | | 3 | 3 | 3 | | 3 | 5 | 1 | 2 | 3 | |
Jin gle Bells Jin gle Bells Jin gle all the way

| 4 | 4 | 4 | 4 | 4 | 3 | 3 | 3 | 3 | 3 | 2 | 2 | 3 | 2 | 5 |
Oh what fun it is to ride in a one horse o pen sleigh Hey

| 3 | 3 | 3 | | 3 | 3 | 3 | | 3 | 5 | 1 | 2 | 3 | |
Jin gle Bells Jin gle Bells Jin gle all the way

| 4 | 4 | 4 | 4 | 4 | 3 | 3 | 3 | 3 | 5 | 5 | 4 | 2 | 1 |
Oh what fun it is to ride in a one horse o pen sleigh

This next song has what's called a pick-up measure, meaning we start counting on a beat other than one!

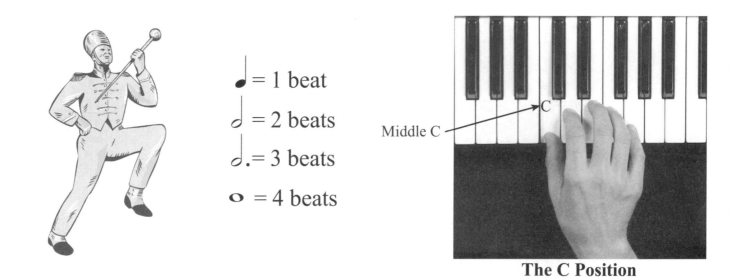

♩ = 1 beat

♩ = 2 beats

♩. = 3 beats

𝅝 = 4 beats

Middle C

The C Position

Oh When The Saints

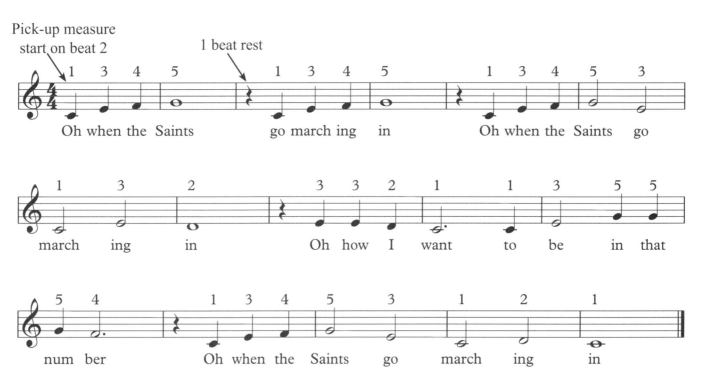

Pick-up measure start on beat 2

1 beat rest

Oh when the Saints   go march ing   in   Oh when the Saints   go

march ing   in   Oh how   I   want   to   be   in   that

num ber   Oh when the Saints   go   march ing   in

The Right Hand Shift

This time, we're going to shift hand positions slightly within the song. Watch out for the fingering here. Note the shifts ahead of time. In Position 2, all of our right hand fingers have moved one key to the right.

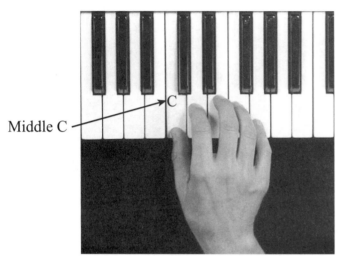

The C Position

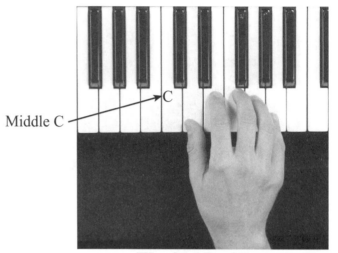

The 2nd Position

Twinkle Twinkle Little Star

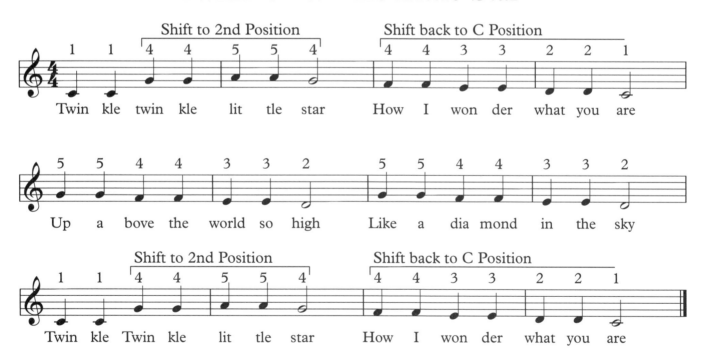

FUN FACT

Twinkle Twinkle Little Star has the same melody as the ABC song. Try singing the ABC song along with the piano part.

Let's do another song with that shift. We'll start in regular position and shift midway through the song.

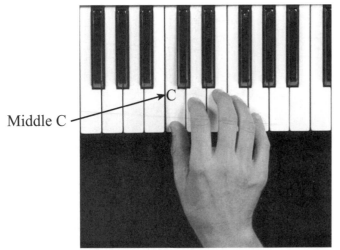

Middle C

The C Position

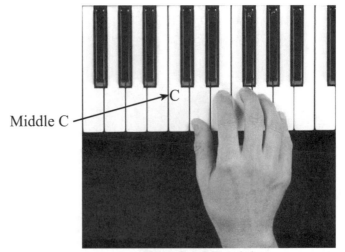

Middle C

The 2nd Position

Rain, Rain, Go Away

Shift

| 5 | 3 | 5 | 5 | 3 | 4 | 4 | 2 | 5 | 4 | 4 | 2 |

Rain, rain, go a way come a gain a noth er day

Shift back

| 4 | 4 | 2 | 2 | 4 | 4 | 2 | 5 | 4 | 3 | 2 | 3 | 1 | 1 |

Lit tle child ren want to play rain___ rain___ go a way

Here's another song with that same shift, a famous old nursery rhyme!

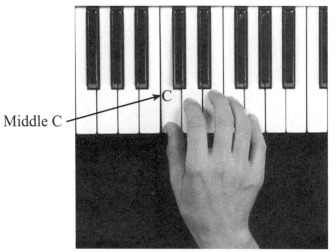

The C Position

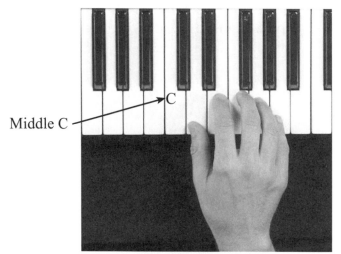

The 2nd Position

This Old Man

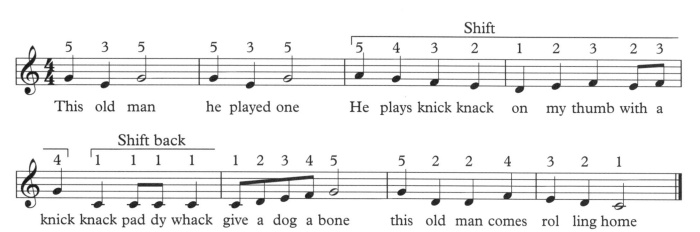

This old man   he played one   He plays knick knack   on   my thumb with a

knick knack pad dy whack give a dog a bone   this old man comes rol ling home

17

The Left Thumb

Our next song is going to use the thumb of your left hand as part of the melody. So put both hands in the C position.

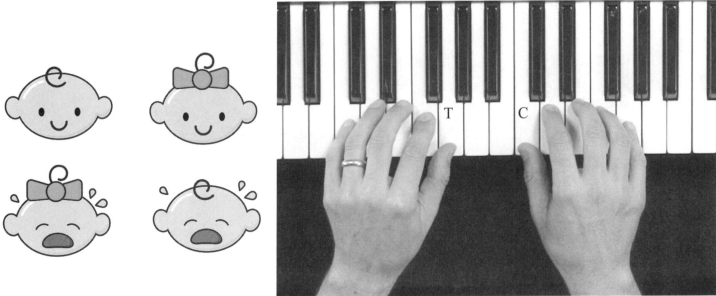

Left & Right Hand C Position

Hush Little Baby

Left Thumb

T	3	3	3	4	3	2	2	2
Hush	lit	tle	ba	by	don't	say	a	word

T	T	2	2	2	2	3	2	1	1
Pa	pa's	gon	na	buy	you	a	mock	ing	bird

18

The G Position

This one is in the G Position, still using the thumb of the left hand as part of the melody. Both hands will move four keys to the right. Your left thumb is on D and your right thumb is on G. Look at the picture to see where your hands go.

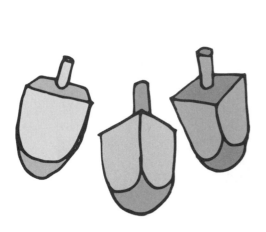

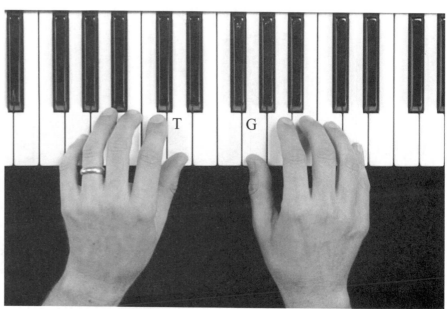

Left & Right Hand G Position

Pick-up measure
start on beat 4

I Have A Little Dreidel

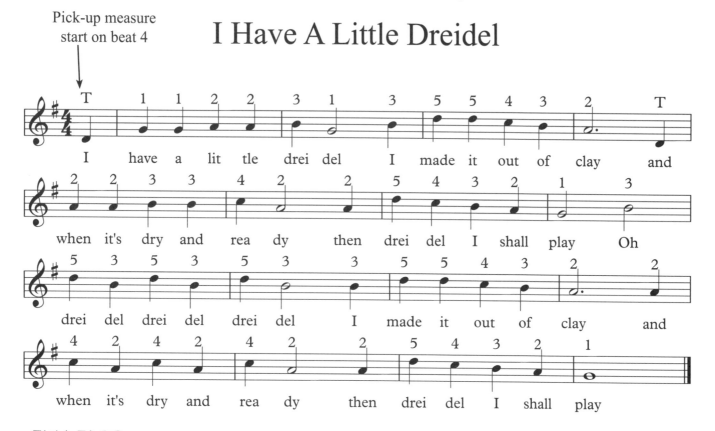

FUN FACT

Did you know a dreidel is a type of spinning top?

19

The Reach

Our next song is a French nursery rhyme. We'll use the left thumb in the last two measures. Once we shift to Position 2 in the 2nd line, we don't shift back. Instead, you'll just reach with your right thumb for that middle C.

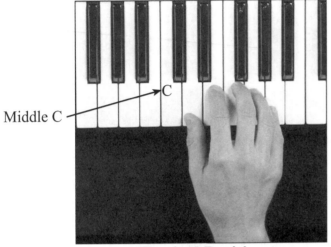

Middle C

The 2nd Position

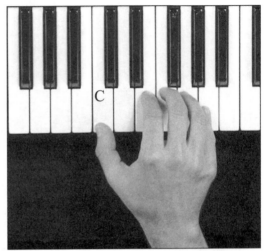

The 2nd Position Reach

Frere Jacques

FUN FACT

This song is about a man who has overslept. What did he miss? He was supposed to ring the morning bell. Oops!

For our next song, we need a new note: a dotted quarter note (♩.). First, let's play *Mary Had A Little Lamb,* but instead of singing the words, count the rhythm out loud.

Quarter Note Exercise

Eighth Note Exercise

Let's do that again , but add in some extra eighth notes. We count these with an "and" in between the beats.

Dotted Quarter Note Exercise

A dotted quarter note takes up the beat following, leaving only the "and" for an eighth note to pick up. Try again. This might feel a little weird at first!

Kind of fun, right? We would say this song "swings" a little bit. If you feel brave, try to play the rest of the song in this same swing fashion.

Let's do our song now. Remember *Ode to Joy?* Well, we kind of cheated before and only used quarter notes. Let's do it the right way now with dotted quarters!

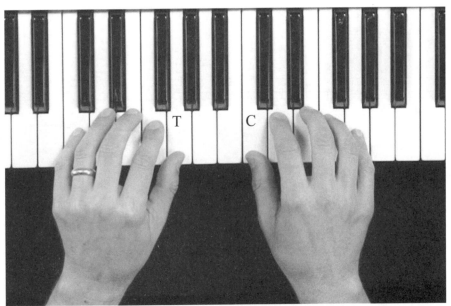

Left & Right Hand C Position

Ode To Joy

Let's do another song with dotted quarter notes. We start in the C Position and shift up one note in the 2nd line, then shift back down again. Try to sing the French!

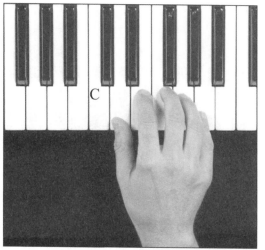

The 2nd Position

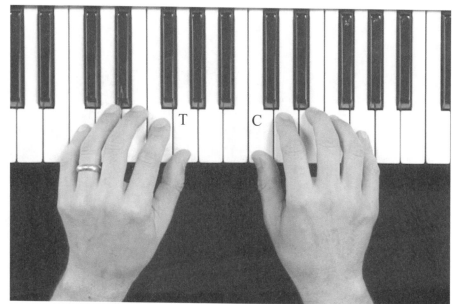

Left & Right Hand C Position

Alouette

23

The next song is a little bit more difficult. It has three different hand positions and a thumb reach. The first position is regular C, but up a whole octave on the piano. No big deal, but it might feel a little weird to start with your hands so far apart.

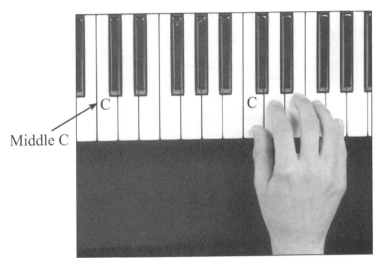

Middle C

The C Position Up 1 Octave

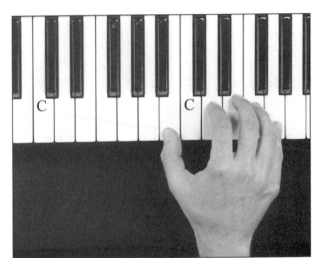

The C Position Up 1 Octave Reach

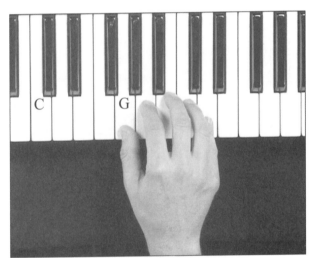

The G Position

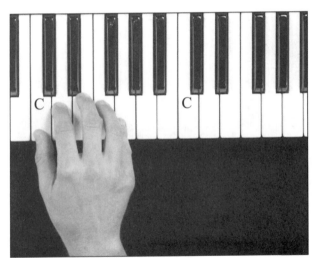

The C Position

That's a lot of hand movement, so make sure your practice these positions before you try to play along with *Yankee Doodle*.

Yankee Doodle

The Bass Clef

Let's take a big step here and use more of our left hand. We'll give our left hand fingers number names as well. Our pinky will be on the next C to the left of middle C.

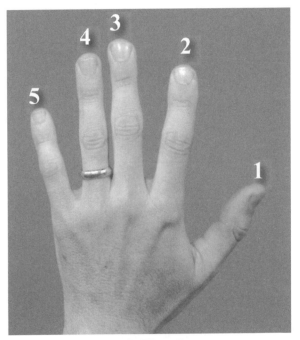

Left Hand

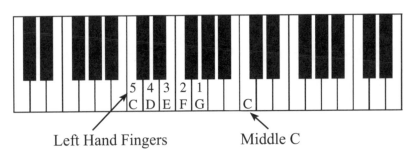

Left Hand Fingers   Middle C

Exercise 10

Let's try using all five fingers of the left hand. This staff is called the bass clef and is for the left hand.

The Grand Staff

Our music notation will now contain two sets of lines or staves. The treble clef is on top and tells your right hand what to play. The bass clef is on bottom and tells your left hand what to play.

      = Treble clef or right hand

      = Bass Clef or left hand

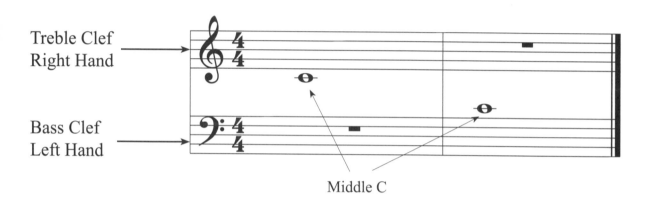

Treble Clef
Right Hand

Bass Clef
Left Hand

Middle C

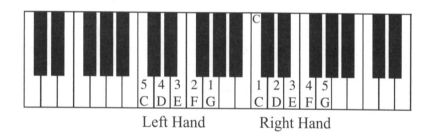

Left Hand   Right Hand

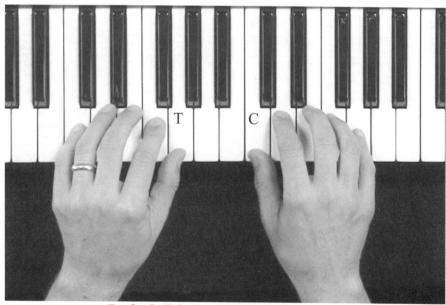

Left & Right Hand C Position

Oh When The Saints Exercise

We're going to add bass notes to several of the songs we did earlier. Let's try an exercise for *Oh When The Saints* to combine the left hand notes with the right hand notes. Go slowly at first and practice this several times until you can play it perfectly.

Now on to the song. Our right hand will play the same thing we did earlier in this course. Go slowly at first until you get comfortable with it.

Oh When The Saints

Ode To Joy Exercise

Now for a two handed version of *Ode To Joy*. Let's start with an exercise to practice the new left hand part.

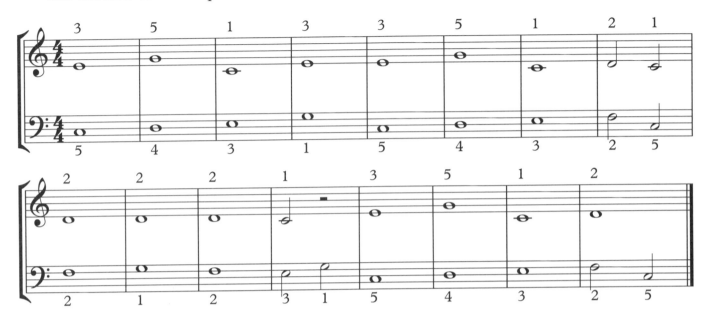

Ode To Joy

Rain, Rain, Go Away Exercise

Now we're going to try playing two notes at the same time with our left hand.

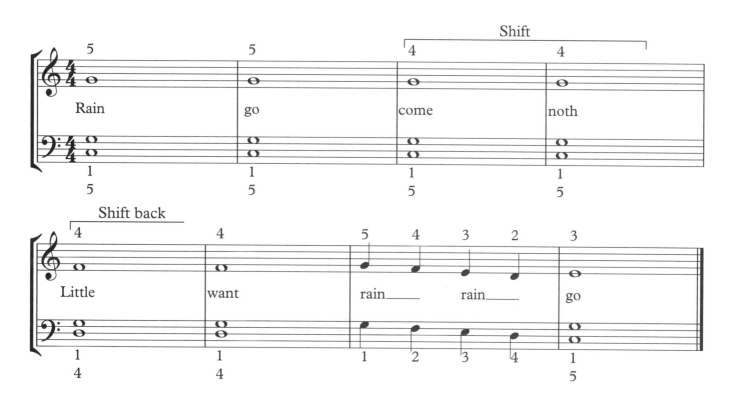

Rain, Rain, Go Away

This Old Man Exercise

We're going to use similar ideas for our two handed version of *This Old Man*.
Let's start by looking at the left hand.

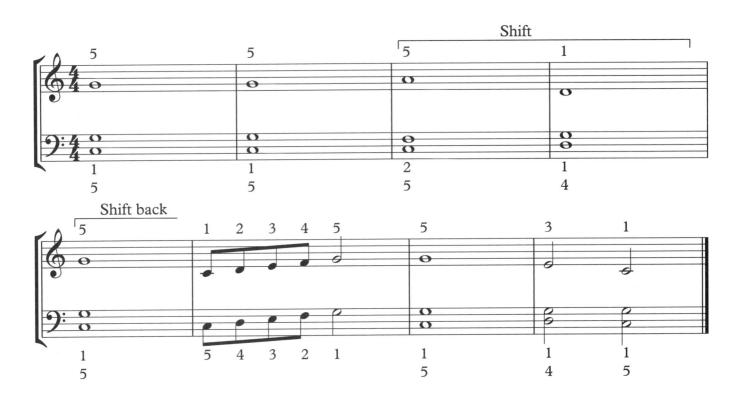

This Old Man

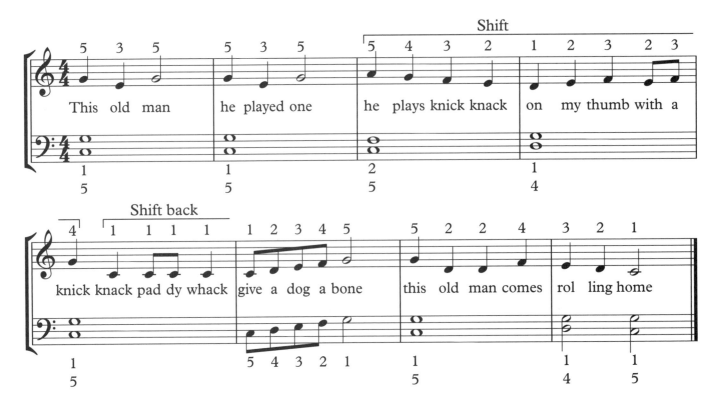

Frere Jacques Exercise

Let's add the left hand part to this French nursery rhyme.

Frere Jacques

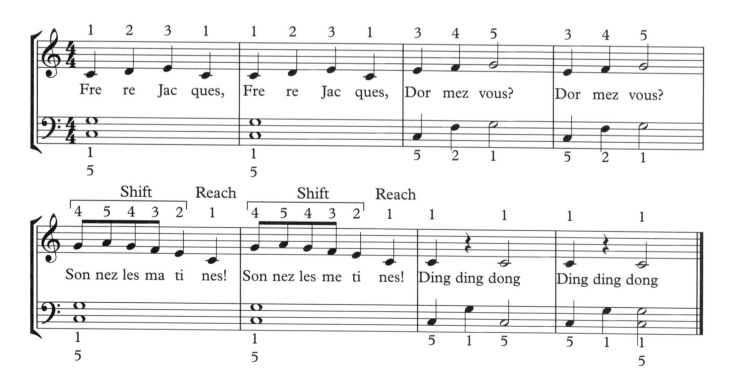

Alouette Exercise

You're probably starting to get the hang of the left hand, but there's one measure
we need to practice before playing the next song, Measure 5.

Alouette

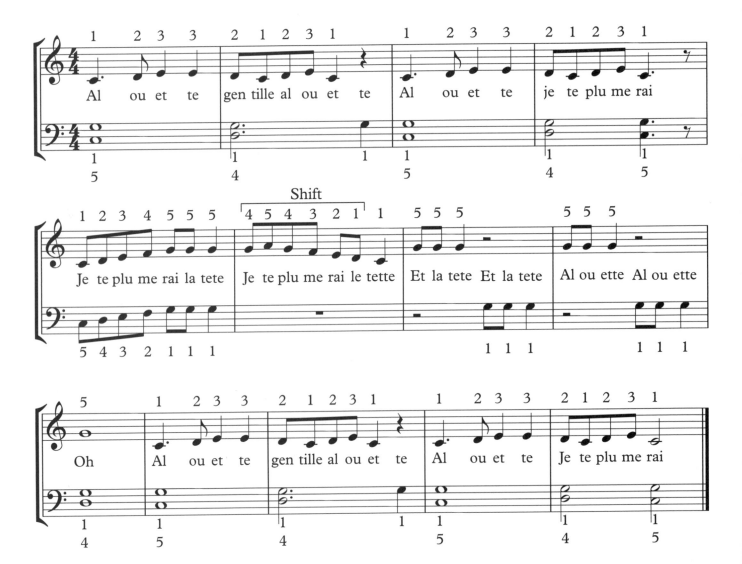

Yankee Doodle Exercise

Let's add the left hand to our last song. We'll use the same right hand melody we learned earlier. It's pretty trick, so make sure you practice along with the video.

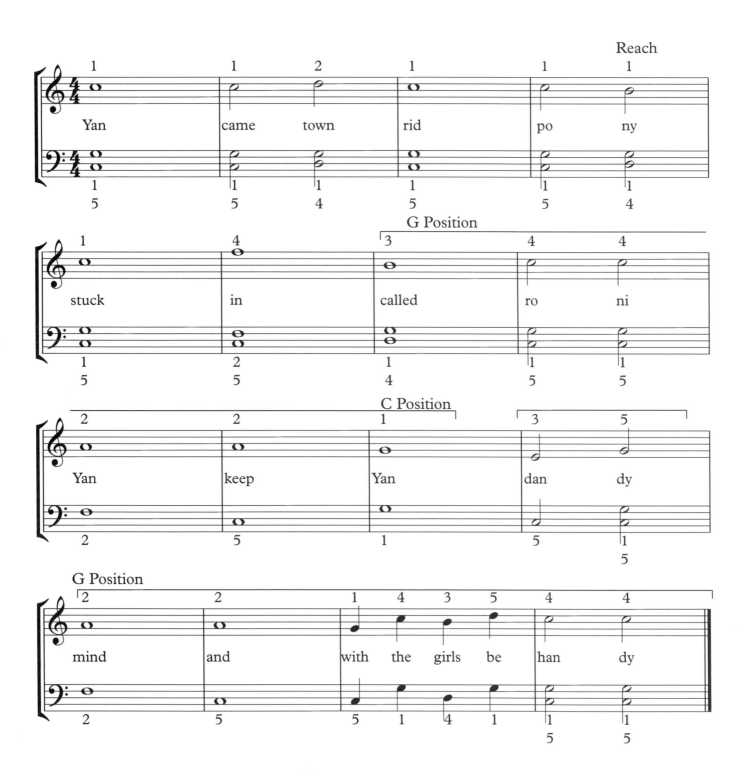

Yankee Doodle

Bonus Information

Congratulations on finishing the song portion of this course. As you keep playing piano, there are additional concepts you'll have to learn. At the start of this book, we discussed how numbers can show you which fingers to play with.

These notes also have letter names. As you start to learn more advanced songs, you may see notation that doesn't include the numbers or letters.

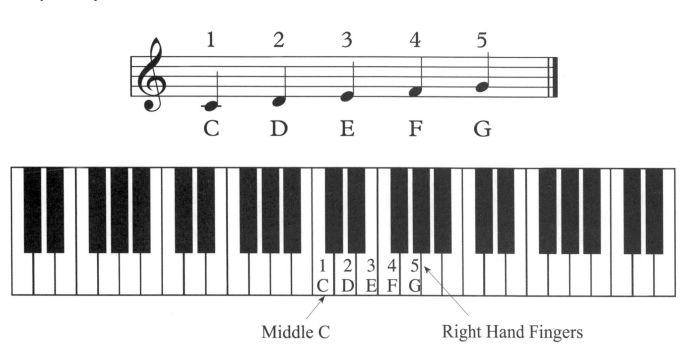

We can use the songs we've learned in this course to start memorizing these note names. Let's play *Mary Had A Little Lamb* again. This time, say the note names to yourself as you play through the song.

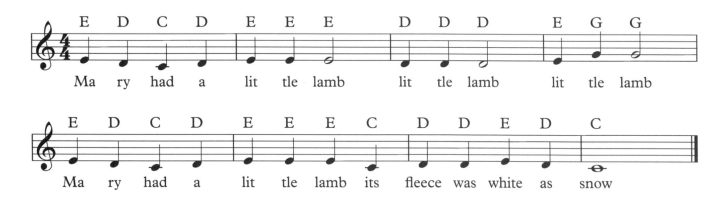

37

Now let's try the same thing with our first version of *Ode To Joy.*

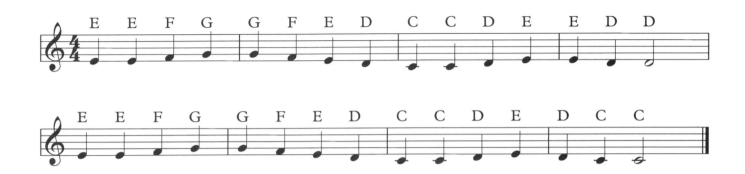

So we've started learning the right hand notes, but we have to cover the left hand as well.

     𝄞 = Treble clef or right hand

     𝄢 = Bass Clef or left hand

Treble Clef
Right Hand

Bass Clef
Left Hand

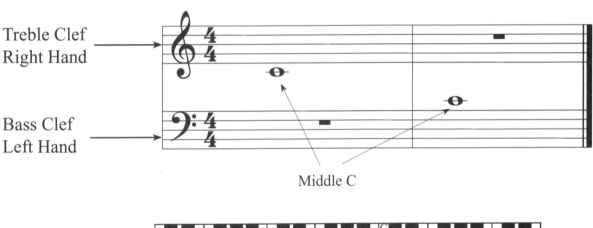

Middle C

Now we'll try reading the notes with the left hand.

Bass Clef
Left Hand

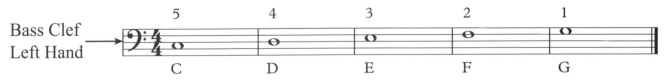

38

Let's try playing the two hand version of *Ode To Joy* using the note names.

It may take a little while to get used to reading the note names and knowing where to place your fingers. Once you learn it though, it's a really useful and necessary skill to have.

Now let's review and learn some new ideas about music notation.

The Treble Clef

The Musical Alphabet consists of just 7 letters:

A-B-C-D-E-F-G

To read music we must be able to find these notes on the staff. The staff is a system of 5 lines and 4 spaces telling you which notes to play. The symbol to the left is called the Clef. We'll start with the Treble Clef. It tells you what each line and space means, kind of like the key to a map.

When music is written in the treble clef, the 5 lines represent these notes:

E G B D F

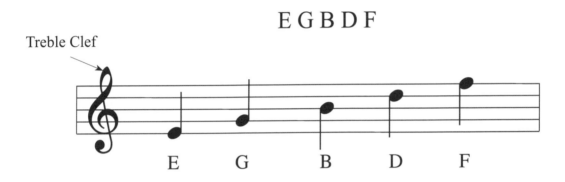

You can remember this by the phrase *Every Good Boy Does Fine*.

The spaces represent the letters:

F A C E

Remember the word FACE. You should memorize these notes and their location on the staff.

The C Major Scale

We can now learn our first scale. Scales are important because all the melodies and chords you hear in songs are made from scales. The first scale you will learn is the C Major Scale. The C Major scale simply uses all the white keys on the keyboard, starting on C and ending on another C an octave higher.

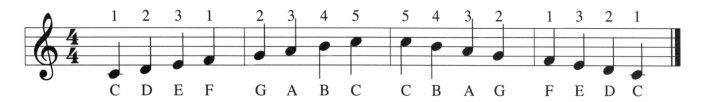

In order to play this scale with the right hand, you must first learn a new technique: crossing the thumb under the third finger.

1. Start with your thumb on middle C and play C, D, and E.

E note

2. Cross your thumb under your 3rd finger and play F, G, A, B, and C.

F note

Thumb crossing under 3rd finger

Play the C major scale forward with your right hand using this technique.

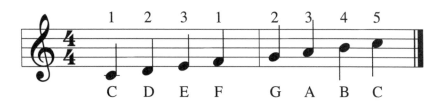

1. Play the C Major Scale backwards, starting with your pinky on the note C - one octave higher than middle C. Play C, B, A, G, and F.

C B A G F   F Note

2. Cross your 3rd finger over your thumb and play E, D, and C.

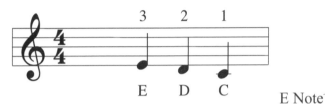

E D C   E Note

Now play the C scale moving down the keyboard.

C B A G F E D C

Practice the C Major Scale forward and backward, using the thumb cross technique you have just learned.

C D E F G A B C   C B A G F E D C

Here is a great exercise for working on the thumb cross. Practice this drill with your right hand over and over.

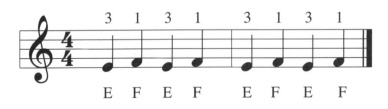

E F E F   E F E F

42

The Bass Clef

The piano uses two clefs. We have already learned the Treble Clef, and now we will learn the Bass Clef. Generally, the right hand will play the treble clef and the left hand will play the bass clef.

The lines in the bass clef represent the notes G B D F and A. Think *Good Birds Don't Fly Away*.

Bass Clef

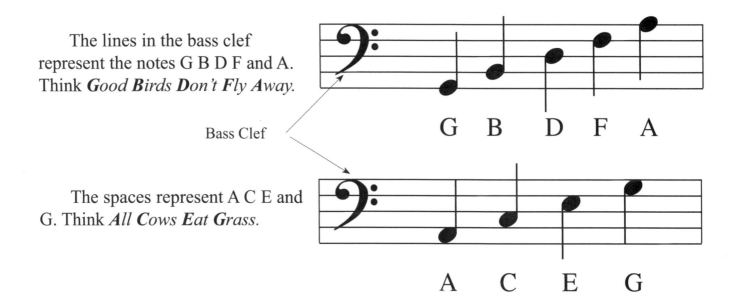

The spaces represent A C E and G. Think *All Cows Eat Grass*.

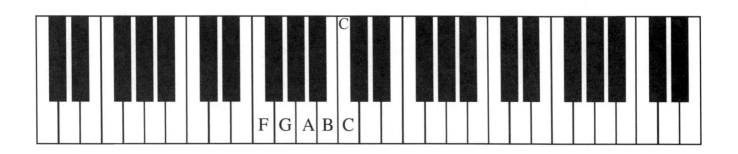

Middle C

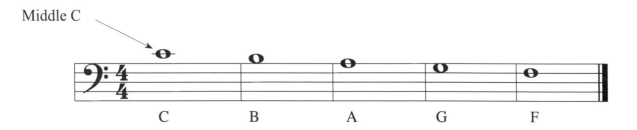

Memorize these 5 notes in the Bass Clef.

C Major Scale - Left Hand

Let's play the C Major Scale using the left hand.

1. Start with your thumb on middle C and play C, B, and A.

A note

2. Cross your thumb under your third finger and play G, F, E, D, and C.

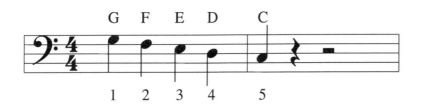

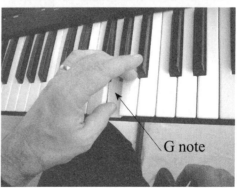
G note

Play the C Major Scale backwards with the left hand. Start on middle C, using the left thumb.

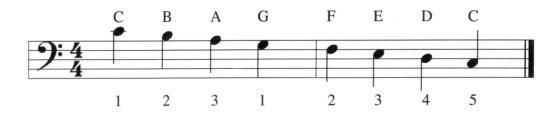

Now play the C Major scale forward starting with your left hand pinky on the note C, one octave below middle C.

1. Start with your pinky on the note C and play C, D, E, F, and G.

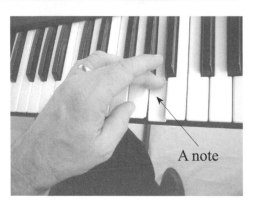

G note

2. Cross your 3rd finger over your thumb and play A, B, and C.

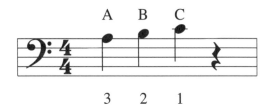

A note

Play the C Major Scale forward with your left hand, starting on the note C one octave below middle C. Use the technique you just learned.

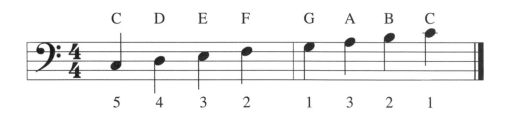

Let's try the cross over exercise using the left hand.

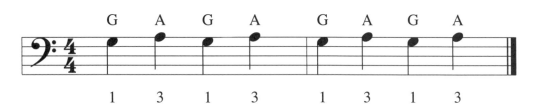